THE
MAGICAL
BOOK OF
SPELLS

FOR HARRY POTTER FANS

Production & publishing:

BoD - Books on Demand, Norderstedt, Germany

ISBN: 9783741273377

1st Edition

Contents – I

ACCIO	PAGE	5
AGUAMENTI	PAGE	6
ALOHOMORA	PAGE	7
ANAPNEO	PAGE	8
APARECIUM	PAGE	9
AVADA KEDAVRA	PAGE	10
AVIS	PAGE	13
CAVE INIMICUM	PAGE	14
COLLOPORTUS	PAGE	15
CRUCIO	PAGE	16
DEFODIO	PAGE	18
DELETRIUS	PAGE	19
DENSAUGEO	PAGE	20
DEPRIMO	PAGE	21
DESCENDO	PAGE	22
DIFFINDO	PAGE	23
DISSENDIUM	PAGE	24
DURO	PAGE	25
ENERVATE	PAGE	26
ENGORGIO	PAGE	27
EPISKEY	PAGE	28
ERECTO	PAGE	29
EVANESCO	PAGE	30
EXPECTO PATRONUM	PAGE	31
EXPELLIARMUS	PAGE	33
EXPULSO	PAGE	34
FERULA	PAGE	35
FINITE	PAGE	36
FINITE INCATATEM	PAGE	37

Contents – II

FLAGRATE	PAGE	38
FURNUNCULUS	PAGE	39
GLISSEO	PAGE	40
HOMENUM REVELIO	PAGE	41
IMPEDIMENTA	PAGE	42
IMPERIO	PAGE	43
IMPERVIUS	PAGE	45
INCARCERUS	PAGE	46
INCENDIO	PAGE	47
LANGLOCK	PAGE	48
LEGILIMENS	PAGE	49
LEVICORPUS	PAGE	50
LIBERACORPUS	PAGE	51
LOCOMOTOR	PAGE	52
LOCOMOTOR MORTIS	PAGE	53
LUMOS	PAGE	54
METEOLOHEX RECANTO	PAGE	55
MOBILCORPUS	PAGE	56
MOBILIARBUS	PAGE	57
MORSMORDRE	PAGE	58
MUFFLIATO	PAGE	59
NOX	PAGE	60
OBLIVIATE	PAGE	61
OBSCURO	PAGE	63
OPPUGNO	PAGE	64
ORCHIDEUS	PAGE	65
PESKIWICHTELI PESTERNOMI	PAGE	66
PETRIFICUS TOTALUS	PAGE	67

Contents – III

PIERTOTUM LOCOMOTOR	PAGE	68
PORTUS	PAGE	69
PRIOR INCANTADO	PAGE	70
PROTEGO	PAGE	71
PROTEGO HORRIBILIS	PAGE	72
PROTEGO TOTALUM	PAGE	73
QUIETUS	PAGE	74
REDUCIO	PAGE	75
REDUCTO	PAGE	76
RELASCHIO	PAGE	77
RENERVATE	PAGE	78
REPARO	PAGE	79
REPELLO MUGGELTUM	PAGE	80
RICTUSEMPRA	PAGE	81
RIDDIKULUS	PAGE	82
SALVIO HEXIA	PAGE	83
SCOURGIFY	PAGE	84
SECTUMSEMPRA	PAGE	85
SERPENSORTIA	PAGE	86
SILENCIO	PAGE	87
SONORUS	PAGE	88
SPECIALIS REVELIO	PAGE	89
STUPEFY	PAGE	90
TARNTALLEGRA	PAGE	91
TERGEO	PAGE	92
WADDIWASI	PAGE	93
WINGARDIUM LEVIOSA	PAGE	94
REFERENCES	PAGE	97

Accio

Latin: accire - to summon; accio - I summon, send for

With "Accio" a witch or wizard can summon objects to them.

This spell appears for the first time during the Quidditch World Cup in the fourth book, when Fred and George try to bring Ton-Tongue Toffees with them from home. Mrs. Weasley uses "Accio" to empty their pockets.

During the first task of the Triwizard Tournament Harry Potter uses this spell to summon his Firebolt, to gain an advantage over the dragon. But he had only used the spell for the first time the day before, so he didn't manage to cast it perfectly or straight away.

AGUAMENTI

Latin: menti - of the mind

A witch or wizard uses "Aguamenti" to conjure up water.

This spell is taught to sixth-years at Hogwarts. Harry uses it twice on the same day: first he tries to conjure up water for Dumbledore in the cave where Dumbledore has supposedly found a Horcrux. Dumbledore had to drink a cup full of potion which he thought the Horcrux was hidden beneath. The potion made him thirsty and Harry tried to fill the goblet with water, but this was prevented by the enchantment on the goblet.

When Death Eaters set fire to Hagrid's hut, Harry helped to extinguish it by using the "Aguamenti" spell.

ALOHOMORA

Latin: mora - obstacle

This spell is used to get around obstacles. Mostly it is used to open doors or locks.

"Alohomora" is the first spell that is mentioned by name in the series. When Hermione, Harry, Ron and Neville are fleeing from the caretaker Mr. Filch at night, Hermione uses this spell to open a locked door at the end of the Forbidden Corridor, so that she and the three others can hide in safety there. Behind the door Fluffy the three-headed dog guards the trapdoor below which the Sorcerer's Stone is kept.

ANAPNEO

"Apnea" - when somebody stops breathing

The spell "Anapneo" is used for example when somebody is choking on something.

In the sixth book Horace Slughorn rushes to the aid of Marcus Belby, who is choking on a piece of pheasant.

APARECIUM

Latin: apertus - unlocked, accessible; parere - to appear, be visible

This spell can make invisible ink visible again.

In the second book Hermione uses the spell to try to find out what is written in Tom Riddle's diary. Unfortunately, it doesn't work.

Avada Kedavra ***

Latin: a - of, from; vadere - to walk, go, change; a vade - go from (command); cadaver - corpse

*** This is one of the Unforgivable Curses.

This spell could also derive from the well-known "Abracadabra", which in turn could come from the Arabic "abreq ad habra". This translates roughly as "the thunder that kills".

Scared by the prophecy that Harry is the one who can defeat him, Lord Voldemort started looking for Harry, and finally found him when Harry was a year old. His father James blocked Voldemort's way and was killed by him. Lily Potter tried to protect Harry and begged Voldemort for mercy. He ordered her to move aside, and when she remained between him and Harry he killed her too. Her sacrifice formed a magical shield around Harry, and when Voldemort aimed a Killing Curse at him, it rebounded and hit Voldemort himself instead. Voldemort was almost killed, lost all his power and was forced to flee.

In the fourth book Harry sees, for the first time since Voldemort killed his parents, how a living being is killed – in Defense Against the Dark Arts, which is taught that year by Alastor Moody (in reality Bartemius Crouch Junior disguised using Polyjuice Potion). He demonstrates the Unforgivable Curses on a spider. When he uses the Killing Curse, there is a bolt of green light and the spider lies dead on the table. Harry also witnesses the death of Cedric Diggory, his fellow champion in the Triwizard Tournament, killed by Peter Pettigrew. The curse doesn't reappear until the end of the fifth book. Voldemort tries once again to kill Harry, but fails this time too. One of the most terrible murders of the series takes place at the end of the sixth book. Albus Dumbledore, the famous headmaster of Hogwarts, is killed by Severus Snape, after being cornered by a group of Death Eaters. It is later revealed that Dumbledore's murder by Snape was planned, because Dumbledore didn't want Draco Malfoy to have to kill him. At the end of the seventh book Harry learns that he himself is one of Voldemort's Horcruxes. This means that Voldemort cannot be killed as long as Harry is alive.

By sacrificing himself, Harry hopes to protect the others, who would otherwise have died for him.

This time Voldemort seems to succeed in killing Harry. What he doesn't know is that in doing so he has destroyed a part of his own soul, and Harry has not been completely killed. He is simply freed of Voldemort's soul, and so he survives.

*The curses Avada Kedavra, Imperio and Crucio are the Unforgivable Curses. This means that their use on other human beings by a witch or wizard is unforgivable and is punished by the Ministry of Magic with a life sentence in Azkaban.

AVIS

Latin: avis - bird

The spell "Avis" makes birds fly out of the tip of a wand.

In the fourth book Mr. Ollivander calibrates Viktor Krum's wand using this spell, making birds fly out of the tip.

CAVE INIMICUM

Latin: roughly: safe refuge

This protective spell can be used, for example, to protect your camp from intruders.

In the seventh book it is used by Harry, Ron and Hermione to protect their various campsites.

COLLOPORTUS

Latin: porta - door, gate

This spell can be used to magically seal a door so that it can only be opened again using "Alohomora".

In the fifth book Hermione, Ginny, Neville and Luna are running away from the Death Eaters in the Ministry. As they run, they try to shake off the Death Eaters using this spell.

CRUCIO ***

Latin: cruciare - to torture; crucio - I torture

*** This is one of the Unforgivable Curses. ***

When this curse is used on someone, it causes them to suffer indescribable torture, which can even drive them mad.

Even though the use of this curse is strictly forbidden, Voldemort and the Death Eaters use it to torture other people and so to obtain information or confessions from them.

The effects of the curse are demonstrated on a spider by Bartemius Crouch Junior (disguised as Alastor Moody) in the fourth book.

The sight of the spider being tortured almost makes Neville collapse.

The Cruciatus Curse is the reason why Neville was raised by his grandmother.

His real parents were tortured with the curse for so long that they were driven mad, by Bellatrix Lestrange together with other Death Eaters, who are imprisoned in Azkaban in punishment for this.

The reason they did this was that the Death Eaters believed that the Longbottoms knew where Lord Voldemort was. They wanted to get this information using torture.

In the fourth book Harry himself is tortured by Lord Voldemort and experiences firsthand how the curse feels.

After Bellatrix Lestrange kills Sirius Black in the fifth book, Harry tries to use the curse on her himself, but he realizes that the effect is a lot weaker when he uses it than when Bellatrix does.

The reason for this is explained at the time, but Harry doesn't understand it until in the seventh book. When you use the Cruciatus Curse, you have to really mean it for its effect to be fully felt.

*The curses Avada Kedavra, Imperio and Crucio are the Unforgivable Curses. This means that their use on other human beings by a witch or wizard is unforgivable and is punished by the Ministry of Magic with a life sentence in Azkaban.

DEFODIO

Latin: defodio - I dig up, dig out, excavate

This spell is used, for example, to widen underground passages.

When Harry, Hermione and Ron break out of Gringotts in the seventh book, they use the spell "Defodio". They are riding a dragon and use the spell to help them break free of the building.

DELETRIUS

Latin: delere - to destroy

Deletrius is the counter-spell to "Prior Incantato". It makes the shadowy shape that has been conjured up disappear again.

In the fourth book, after Amos Diggory has shown that the Dark Mark was cast with Harry's wand, he uses this counter-spell to make the shadow of the Dark Mark disappear again.

Densaugeo

Latin: dens - tooth; augere - to grow; augeo - I make grow

When this spell is cast on somebody, their teeth grow to an abnormal size.

Draco Malfoy uses the spell in the fourth book in a fight with Harry. His spell was deflected by a "Furnunculus" spell from Harry's wand and hit Hermione instead. This made her teeth grow to such an enormous size that she had to be taken to the Hospital Wing. Her teeth were fixed there so that they shrunk back to their normal size.

DEPRIMO

Latin: deprimo - I lower, sink

In the seventh book, Hermione uses this spell to blast a hole in the floor of the Lovegoods' living room, after Xenophilius Lovegood betrays the trio to the Death Eaters. This allows them to escape.

DESCENDO

Latin: descendere - to go down; descendo - I bring down

In the seventh book Ron uses this spell to bring down a ladder from the attic, where he wants to show Harry a magical ghoul.

During the Battle of Hogwarts the spell is also used by Crabbe in the Room of Requirement.

DIFFINDO

Latin: diffindere - to split; diffindo - I split

This spell can tear or rip the object it is aimed at.

When Harry learns about the first task of the Triwizard Tournament in the fourth book, he wants to let Cedric know about it. He uses the spell to tear Cedric's bag so that he can talk to him while Cedric picks his things up off the floor.

Harry also uses the spell in the sixth book. He swaps the cover of his new copy of "Advanced Potion-Making" with the cover of the Half-Blood Prince's copy. To reattach the ripped-off covers, he uses the spell "Reparo".

DISSENDIUM

Latin: dissensio - disagreement, discord

This spell is able to open one of the secret passages to Hogsmeade. On the Marauder's Map that Harry is given by Fred and George in the third book, all the secret passages that lead to Hogsmeade are shown. One of them finishes right in Honeydukes. The entrance is under the humped back of a statue of a one-eyed witch. If you tap your wand on the hump and say "Dissendium", it opens, and you can climb into the secret passage.

Harry is actually forbidden from going to Hogsmeade, which is why he is forced to use the secret passages, which he does several times.

DURO

Spanish: duro - hard

This spell is able to turn objects hard. In the seventh book Hermione uses it while they are escaping from a group of Death Eaters. She turns a tapestry into a stone wall to hold the Death Eaters up.

ENERVATE

"to enervate" - to weaken
(Probably means that the original spell will be weakened.)

This spell is used to wake up somebody who has been Stunned using "Stupefy". After the house elf Winky has been Stunned in the fourth book, she is woken up again by Amos Diggory using this spell.

Dumbledore also uses it to wake up the Stunned Viktor Krum after he and Harry find Krum at the edge of the Forbidden Forest.

ENGORGIO

"to engorge" - to swell

This spell is used to enlarge animals, for example. The animal that the spell is used on grows to a considerable size.

To show the students the Unforgivable Curses more clearly in Defense Against the Dark Arts, Bartemius Crouch Junior (disguised as Alastor Moody using Polyjuice Potion) uses the spell to enlarge a spider. The counter-spell to "Engorgio" is "Reducio".

EPISKEY

Greek: episkeyazo - to repair, mend

This spell can heal broken bones very quickly. You aim your wand at the relevant place and say "Episkey" and the fracture is healed within a matter of seconds.

The spell is only mentioned by name a few times in the books. In the sixth book Tonks heals Harry's nose after Draco Malfoy breaks it on the Hogwarts Express. Harry only lets her heal it out of politeness.

But he takes note of the spell and uses it during a Quidditch training session when Ron accidentally punches Demelza Robins in the face. Harry uses the spell to heal her mouth.

The spell was probably used frequently by Madame Pomfrey in the earlier books, for example to heal broken wrists.

ERECTO

Latin: erectus - upright (standing); erigo - I set up, put up

Hermione uses this spell in the seventh book to put up their tent at the first campsite. The spell ensures that the tent puts itself up completely, with guy ropes and tent pegs.

EVANESCO

Latin: evanesco - I make disappear

If you aim your wand at an object or a liquid and say "Evanesco", it disappears in the blink of an eye.

Bill Weasley uses the spell in the fifth book after a meeting of the Order of the Phoenix. A few rolls of parchment have accidentally been left lying around and he uses the spell to make them disappear.

The spell is also often used by Professor Snape to Vanish potions made by his students.

Expecto Patronum

Latin: expectare - to wait for; expecto - I wait for; patronus - protector
(Sentence: I'm waiting for a protector.)

The Patronus Charm is the only really effective defense against a Dementor attack. It is one of the most difficult spells to cast. When it is used correctly, it creates a Patronus, a projection of happiness and hope that has a different form for every witch and wizard. However, in the books the Patronus is always an animal. What makes the spell so difficult is that the witch or wizard must think of a very happy memory in order to successfully conjure up a Patronus. Dementors feed on the happiness of their victims, so it is difficult to concentrate on something happy in the presence of a Dementor.

In the third book, when Dementors on the Quidditch pitch make Harry lose a match, he makes Professor Lupin teach him how to defend himself against Dementors. Lupin gets hold of a Boggart for their lessons, because it would hardly be possible to practice the spell on a real Dementor. On only his third try, Harry manages to hold the Dementor off briefly with a silvery mist (the Boggart takes the shape of a Dementor for Harry). On his first two tries he passed out. But he is unsatisfied with his result.

Towards the end of the third book, Hermione and Harry travel in time three hours into the past. He sees his past self being attacked by Dementors. With a perfectly conjured Patronus that takes the shape of a stag, he manages to save Hermione and Sirius Black's lives as well as his own.

The spell is also used by the Order of the Phoenix to send important messages.

EXPELLIARMUS

Latin: expellere - to expel, drive out; expello - I expel; arma - weapons

Expelliarmus is the Disarming Charm.

The spell is mentioned by name for the first time in the second book, when Professor Snape faces Gilderoy Lockhart at the Duelling Club. When he casts "Expelliarmus" at Lockhart, Lockhart's wand isn't just knocked out of his hand. Lockhart is knocked off his feet and into the air by the spell, showing him up in front of the whole school.

Harry and his friends use this spell frequently in the later books.

Expulso

Latin: expulso - I drive out, drive away

This spell creates a shock wave that blasts objects out of the way.

In the seventh book it is used by Thorfinn Rowle, a Death Eater. He and Dolohov had tracked down Harry, Ron and Hermione after they fled to a cafe on Tottenham Court Road. The curse blasted a table into the air and Harry, who was standing behind it, was flung into a wall, causing his Invisibility Cloak to slip down.

FERULA

Latin: ferula - reed, rod, stick

Witches and wizards who can't quite manage the "Episkey" spell can use this one instead. But it only splints the broken bone and numbs the pain, so if possible a witch or wizard should still be found who can fully heal the bone with "Episkey".

In the third book Professor Lupin uses this spell on Ron's leg, which Sirius Black had broken when he dragged Ron into the Shrieking Shack while in the form of a dog.

Finite

Latin: finite - end! (plural command)

This spell is used to lift minor spells or curses. When a witch or wizard points their wand at the enchanted or cursed people or objects and says "Finite", the spell is lifted in the blink of an eye. But it is not clear whether this spell also helps against Unforgivable Curses and the like.

In the fifth book, Remus Lupin uses the spell to lift the Tarantallegra Curse that had been cast on Neville. Harry also uses it in the seventh book in the Room of Requirement, to rebuild a high pile of objects hidden there that had collapsed when Crabbe hit it with the spell "Descendo".

Finite Incantatem

Latin: finite incantatem! - end the spell! (command)

This spell is very similar to "Finite". It isn't made clear whether the two spells have different effects.

Just like with "Finite", the witch or wizard points their wand at the enchanted people or objects and says "Finite Incantatem" to lift minor spells or curses.

In the second book, Professor Snape uses Finite Incantatem to end all the spells and curses cast at the Duelling Club. In the seventh book, when Ron is ordered to stop the rain in Yaxley's office in the Ministry of Magic, Hermione tells him to use "Finite Incantatem".

FLAGRATE

Latin: flagrare - to burn, blaze

This spell can be used to mark doors. When a witch or wizard points their wand at a door and says "Flagrate", a flaming "X" appears on the door.

In the fifth book Hermione uses this spell to mark the doors they have already opened in the first room of the Ministry of Magic, so that they know which doors they have already tried and which ones they haven't.

FURNUNCULUS

A "furnuncle" - a boil

Saying "Furnunculus" while pointing one's wand at someone causes large blisters to sprout where the spell hits them.

In a confrontation with Draco Malfoy in the fourth book, Harry fires a Furnunculus curse at him to disfigure his face. But the spell is deflected by Malfoy's curse and hits Goyle instead, making large boils grow on his nose.

The Densaugeo curse that Malfoy had cast was also deflected and hit Hermione.

GLISSEO

French: glisser - to slide, glide

This spell causes objects to become slippery and smooth. In the seventh book Hermione uses it to turn a staircase in Hogwarts into a slide, helping her, Ron and Harry to escape the Death Eaters.

HOMENUM REVELIO

Latin: homo: human; revelare: to reveal; Latin: hominem revelo - roughly: I reveal the humans

This spell can be used when somebody wants to know if there is anybody else in the same building. It isn't clear from the books exactly how the presence of other people is revealed.

Hermione uses the spell in the seventh book, for example, in the Blacks' house, to find out whether she, Harry and Ron are alone there. A Death Eater called Selwyn also uses the spell in the seventh book to check if there is anyone else in Mr. Lovegood's house.

While chatting with fans shortly after the seventh book was released, Rowling explained that Harry was sometimes visible to Dumbledore from under his Invisibility Cloak as Dumbledore used this spell.

IMPEDIMENTA

Latin: impedimentum - obstacle; impedire - to impede, hinder, hold back

Somebody who is hit by this spell is drained of energy for a few minutes or is only capable of moving very slowly.

During the third task of the Triwizard Tournament, Harry comes across a Blast-Ended Skrewt and uses the spell to paralyze it.

IMPERIO

Latin: imperare - to command; impero - I command

Imperio is one of the Unforgivable Curses*. It gives the witch or wizard who uses it control over their victim.

In fourth year Alastor Moody (in reality Bartemius Crouch Junior disguised using Polyjuice Potion) teaches Defense Against the Dark Arts. In the class he demonstrates the Unforgivable Curses on a spider, including the Imperius Curse. He makes the spider do various things including somersaults and cartwheels. He also demonstrates the effect of the curse on the students. They all fall completely under his control and can't resist doing what he orders them to do. The only one who manages to resist is Harry. Eventually he even manages to shake off the curse completely. This helps him later in the book. When Voldemort wants to use the curse to make him do something, he can refuse. Before Voldemort disappeared, the curse was used very often by Death Eaters to control other people. In the end, however, it isn't only used by Voldemort's followers. Professor McGonagall uses it on a

Death Eater called Amycus Carrow at the end of the seventh book.

*The curses Avada Kedavra, Imperio and Crucio are the Unforgivable Curses. This means that their use on other human beings by a witch or wizard is unforgivable and is punished by the Ministry of Magic with a life sentence in Azkaban.

IMPERVIUS

"impervious" - watertight, waterproof, impermeable

If a witch or wizard points their wand at an object or similar and says "Impervius", it will become water-repellent. This makes it a useful tool in the books.

In the third book, Hermione uses the spell to make Harry's glasses repel water before a Quidditch match against Hufflepuff in stormy weather and strong rain. This means he can see much better and helps him to do his job as Seeker. Unfortunately, he doesn't manage to catch the Snitch, because Dementors turn up on the pitch just as he catches sight of it and he faints.

INCARCEROUS

"incarcerate" - to lock up, imprison

This spell creates shackles: if a witch or wizard points their wand at a person or animal and says "Incarcerous", the victim is tied up with strong ropes that appear out of nowhere.

Dolores Umbridge uses the spell on a centaur in the fifth book. Harry and Hermione go into the Forbidden Forest with her and come across a herd of centaurs. Umbridge loses control and shackles one of the herd. The rest then chase her into the Forest.

The spell also appears in the third book: Professor Snape uses it to tie up Remus Lupin in the Shrieking Shack. We don't learn the name of the spell at this point since he doesn't say it out loud.

INCENDIO

Latin: incendium - fire; incendere - to set fire to; incendo - I set on fire

This spell is used to create fire without tools. The witch or wizard points their wand at something that can be set on fire, for example a fireplace or a stack of wood, and says "Incendio", and a fire starts in the blink of an eye.

The spell appears for the first time in the fourth book. Mr. Weasley uses it to light a fire in the Dursleys' fireplace, so that he, his children and Harry can use Floo Powder to travel to the Burrow.

The spell is also used by Death Eaters at the end of the sixth book to set Hagrid's hut on fire.

LANGLOCK

Spanish: lengua - tongue

This spell appears in the Half-Blood Prince's Potions book. It makes the victim of the curse unable to speak, because their tongue is stuck to the roof of their mouth.

Harry uses it on Filch and Peeves several times in the sixth book.

Legilimens

Latin: legere - to read; mens - mind

This spell lets a witch or wizard access the thoughts and memories of their victim, so that they can know what their opponent is thinking and feeling.

When Voldemort seems to be using Legilimency to control Harry Potter's thoughts, Albus Dumbledore asks Professor Snape to give Harry lessons in Occlumency. This is the art of resisting a Legilimens and closing one's mind so that an enemy can't break into it. Snape is an expert at both Legilimency and Occlumency, which makes him the best teacher for Harry.

Voldemort is believed to be the greatest Legilimens. Very few people can lie to him without his knowing – only people who have mastered Occlumency.

LEVICORPUS

Latin: levis - light, weightless; corpus - body

This is another spell from the Half-Blood Prince's Potions book. It doesn't need to be said out loud to work. The witch or wizard only needs to think "Levicorpus" and their victim will be hoisted into the air upside-down. Until "Liberacorpus" is used on them, they will stay hanging there no matter how much they try to get back down.

After Harry finds the spell in the Half-Blood Prince's book, he tries it out straight away. But since he has no idea what it does, the sleeping Ron is torn out of bed and suspended in the air in front of Harry. Harry manages to find the counter-charm in the book and lets Ron down again.

LIBERACORPUS

Latin: libera - free; corpus - body

This is another spell from the Half-Blood Prince's Potions book. It is used as the counter-jinx to Levicorpus, to let the person who is hanging upside-down back down to the ground.

After he accidentally hoists Ron into the air by his ankle in the sixth book using Levicorpus, Harry reverses the effect using this spell.

LOCOMOTOR

Latin: locus - place; motor - mover

When it is too difficult for a witch or wizard to carry something, they simply have to point their wand at the object they want to transport and say "Locomotor", followed by the name of the object. This will then start to hover and the witch or wizard can direct it using their wand.

In the fifth book, Tonks uses her wand to transport Harry's trunk downstairs from his room in the Dursleys' house when Harry is being picked up by members of the Order of the Phoenix.

LOCOMOTOR MORTIS

Latin: locus - place; motor - mover; mors - death

This is known as the Leg-Locker Curse. As the name suggests, it's used to stick the victim's legs together. They can then only hop or pull themself forward using their arms.

Draco Malfoy uses this curse on Neville Longbottom in the first book. As Neville doesn't know the counter-curse, he has to hop back to Gryffindor tower, where Hermione can release him.

LUMOS

Latin: lumen - light

This is a very frequently used everyday spell. When the witch or wizard is holding their wand, they only need to say "Lumos" and the tip of the wand will light up like a flashlight.

The spell is used for the first time in the second book, when Harry and Ron follow the spiders into the Forbidden Forest.

When the witch or wizard doesn't need the light anymore, they simply have to say "Nox" and the light will go out again.

METEOLOJINX RECANTO

Italian: meteo - weather forecast
Latin: recanto - I magic away, revoke

This spell can be used to undo weather charms.

In the seventh book Harry, Ron and Hermione break into the Ministry. They are disguised as Ministry employees, which causes problems for Ron. He is disguised as a wizard called Reg Cattermole, who is married to a Muggleborn. A Death Eater called Yaxley threatens to cause even more trouble for his wife if he can't stop the rain in Yaxley's office within an hour. Ron bumps into his father in a lift, and Mr. Weasley advises him to use this spell to solve the problem.

Mobilicorpus

Latin: mobilis - movable; corpus - body

The spell Mobilicorpus can be used to control a lifeless person like a puppet and direct them with wand movements. The witch or wizard only has to point their wand at the person and say "Mobilicorpus". The body will then stand up by itself and can then be moved.

In the third book, Remus Lupin uses this spell to move Professor Snape out of the Shrieking Shack after he has been knocked out.

MOBILIARBUS

Latin: mobilis - movable; arbor - tree

This spell moves an uprooted tree from one place to another. If the witch or wizard points their wand at the tree they want to move and says "Mobiliarbus", the tree levitates a few centimeters off the floor and moves to the desired place.

When Harry sneaks into the Three Broomsticks in Hogsmeade just before Christmas and the Minister of Magic suddenly turns up accompanied by teachers from Hogwarts, Hermione uses this spell to move a Christmas tree in front of their table so that Harry can't be seen.

MORSMORDRE

Latin: mors - death; mordeo - to burn
French: mordre - to bite

The Death Eaters use the spell "Morsmordre" to conjure up the Dark Mark. When the spell is cast, the Mark appears from the tip of the wand and hovers in the sky.

After the Quidditch World Cup final, there is total chaos at the campsite. Harry, Ron and Hermione escape into the woods. They hear someone use this spell to send up a Dark Mark over the campsite.

The house elf Winky is found near where the Mark was cast, and at first she comes under suspicion. In reality, however, it was Bartemius Crouch Junior who cast the Mark.

MUFFLIATO

"muffle" - to cover up or reduce a sound

Harry discovers this spell written in the margin of the Half-Blood Prince's copy of "Advanced Potion-Making". It creates a buzzing noise in the ears of everyone nearby to prevent them from eavesdropping.

Harry uses it several times, including once in the Hospital Wing to ensure that nobody hears him telling Dobby and Kreacher to follow Malfoy. Although Hermione hates it when anyone uses the Half-Blood Prince's spells, she uses Muffliato herself in the seventh book. She casts it wherever she goes with Harry and Ron so that nobody can hear their conversations.

NOX

Latin: nox - night

This is the counter-charm for "Lumos". When a witch or wizard no longer needs the light that they have conjured up with "Lumos", they only need to say "Nox" and the light at the tip of their wand will go out.

In their third year Harry and Hermione use this spell when Ron is dragged into the Shrieking Shack by Sirius and the two follow him.

OBLIVIATE

Latin: oblivio - forgetting

Obliviate is the Memory Charm. It can be used to manipulate or erase somebody's memories. A side effect is that the victim goes cross-eyed and has a blank facial expression for a while.

In the second book Gilderoy Lockhart tries to use the spell on Ron. But he uses Ron's own wand, which had been broken earlier in the book. The spell backfires on Lockhart and he loses his memory.

A Ministry employee uses this spell on Mr. Roberts, a Muggle, to make him forget the events at the Quidditch World Cup. Xenophilius Lovegood's memories are also altered using this spell. In the seventh book he tells Harry, Ron and Hermione the Tale of the Three Brothers and then betrays them to the Death Eaters, because his daughter has been kidnapped and he wants to get her back. Hermione then alters his memory.

Hermione also uses the spell in the seventh book to wipe the memories of two Death Eaters and a waitress. After Harry, Ron and Hermione fled from Bill and Fleur's wedding to a cafe on Tottenham Court Road, they were tracked down there by two Death Eaters. The trio overpowered the Death Eaters and, just to be safe, Hermione erased their memory.

Obscuro

Latin: obscuro - I darken, conceal, hide

The spell "Obscuro" conjures up a blindfold over the face of a person, animal or being that cannot be magically removed, so that the victim can't see anything.

Hermione uses this spell after she has summoned the ex-headmaster Phineas Nigellus into his portrait from the Blacks' house and asked him about Godric Gryffindor's sword. This stops him from seeing who is with Hermione or where they are.

Oppugno

Latin: oppugnare - to attack, storm; oppugno - I attack, storm

This spell causes creatures to attack a person.

Hermione uses it in the sixth book in a fit of jealousy at Ron. She is so upset by Ron's relationship with Lavender that she sets a swarm of birds on him after Gryffindor's first Quidditch match.

ORCHIDEOUS

The spell "Orchideous" makes a bunch of
flowers burst out of the tip of the wand.

In the fourth book, Mr. Ollivander is calibrating
the wands of the Triwizard Tournament
champions. He casts this spell with Fleur
Delacour's wand to conjure up a bunch of
flowers for her.

Peskipiksi Pesternomi

This spell could be derived from a sentence: "Pesky pixie, pester no me".

The spell is apparently used to bring pixies under control. Gilderoy Lockhart tries it out on a gang of rampaging pixies in their second year, but it doesn't have any effect. However, it isn't clear whether this is because the spell is wrong or because of Lockhart's incompetence in using it.

PETRIFICUS TOTALUS

Latin: petra - stone; totalis - completely
"petrify" - to freeze, turn to stone

This is the Full Body-Bind Curse, a step up from the Leg-Locker Curse. The spell causes the victim's whole body to be "petrified" or frozen so that they can only move their eyes, until they are released by the counter-curse.

Hermione uses this curse on Neville Longbottom in their first year, when he tries to stop her leaving the Gryffindor tower with Harry and Ron at night. At that point Neville didn't know that the trio were trying to find the Sorcerer's Stone and thought he needed to stop them.

Harry and his friends use this spell very often in the later books while fighting Voldemort's Death Eaters.

PIERTOTUM LOCOMOTOR

French: pierre - stone
Latin: totus - totally; locus - place; motor -
mover

Professor McGonagall uses this spell before the
Battle of Hogwarts in the seventh book to bring
to life the statues and suits of armor that stand
throughout the castle and order them to defend
the school against Lord Voldemort and his army.

PORTUS

Latin: porta - door, gate, entry; portus - harbor, refuge

Witches and wizards can use Portkeys to travel quickly from one place to another. An object becomes a Portkey when a witch or wizard points their wand at it and says "Portus". A blue light appears briefly and then the object can be used to travel.

After the battle in the Ministry, Dumbledore turns the head of a statue of a wizard into a Portkey so that Harry can travel back to Hogwarts.

Prior Incantato

Latin: prior - previous; incantare - to cast a spell

The last spell that a wand cast can be revealed using "Prior Incantato". The witch or wizard must touch their wand to the tip of the wand in question and say the spell. This conjures up a shadowy form of the last spell cast by the other wand.

This shadowy form can be made to disappear again using "Deletrius".

In the fourth book Amos Diggory uses "Prior Incantato" to show that the wand they have found was used to conjure up a Dark Mark over the campsite at the Quidditch World Cup.

Protego

Latin: protego - I protect

This spell creates an invisible shield against minor to moderate spells and curses. If a witch or wizard is protecting themself with "Protego" and is hit by a curse, this will bounce off the shield and hit the person who cast it with a weakened version of the curse.

Harry learnt to cast this spell when he was preparing for the third task of the Triwizard Tournament in his fourth year at Hogwarts. In his fifth year he then teaches the members of the DA (Dumbledore's Army) how to use it.

However, the wording of the spell only appears during Harry's Occlumency lessons with Professor Snape in the fifth book. Harry manages to resist Snape's attempt to use Legilimency on him by using "Protego". Snape's "Legilimens" is then reversed and Harry has access to Snape's memories.

PROTEGO HORRIBILIS

Latin: roughly: I protect from the terrible thing.

"Protego Horribilis" is an extension of the protective spell "Protego" which is meant in particular for terrible dangers, probably Dark magic. Professor Flitwick uses it in the seventh book to protect Hogwarts when Voldemort and his army attack.

PROTEGO TOTALUM

Latin: protego - I protect; totalis - totally

This is a strong, long-lasting protective spell which is a stronger form of "Protego". Hermione, Harry and Ron use it in the seventh book to protect their tent from intruders.

QUIETUS

from "quiet"

"Quietus" is the counter-charm to "Sonorus". It is used to bring the amplified voice back to a normal volume.

During the Quidditch World Cup in the fourth book, Ludo Bagman first of all used "Sonorus" to magically amplify his voice and then used this spell to speak more quietly again.

REDUCIO

Latin: reduco - I withdraw, pull back

Casting "Reducio" on an object or animal makes it shrink to a smaller size.

In their fourth year, the fake Alastor Moody (really Bartemius Crouch Junior) uses "Engorgio" to enlarge the spider that he demonstrates the Cruciatus Curse on in Defense Against the Dark Arts. He then uses "Reducio" to make it shrink back to the right size.

REDUCTO

from "reduce"

This spell is used to get rid of obstacles. An object that is hit by "Reducto" crumbles to dust or is removed in some other way immediately.

Harry learns this spell when he is preparing for the third task of the Triwizard Tournament in the fourth book. He tries to clear a hedge out of the way in the maze using the spell, but only manages to burn a hole in it.

In his fifth year at Hogwarts, he teaches the DA (Dumbledore's Army) how to use the spell.

In their sixth year, a member of the Order of the Phoenix uses this spell to try to destroy a barrier that the Death Eaters have created at the bottom of the Astronomy Tower, but doesn't manage it.

Relashio

Italian: rilascio - release

"Relashio" is used to forcibly release someone or something. A witch or wizard can use it to free themself from something that is holding onto them. This spell is often very useful in lakes, rivers and the like. "Grindylows" are often found underwater. They grab onto their prey and try to drag them down. A witch or wizard can use "Relashio" to free themself from the water demons.

Harry and the other students probably learn this spell in their third year. In Defense Against the Dark Arts, Professor Lupin brings a Grindylow to class and probably also demonstrates the spell to fight them off. But the name of the spell is only revealed in the fourth book, when Harry is attacked by a Grindylow in the second task of the Triwizard Tournament and uses this spell to break free of it.

RENERVATE

Latin: re - again; nervosus - strong, powerful

The exact effect of this spell is not revealed to the reader. Harry uses it in the sixth book to revive Dumbledore, who seems to be unconscious. But it is not clear whether Dumbledore was really revived by the spell or whether that would have happened anyway without Harry's help.

The spell could come from "Enervate", which is used to wake up people who have been Stunned, but this isn't made clear.

Reparo

Latin: reparare - to repair; reparo - I repair

Witches and wizards don't need to worry about broken objects. With this spell it's simple to repair them. They just have to point their wand at the broken item and say "Reparo" and in the blink of an eye it's as good as new.

In their fourth year, Hermione uses this spell to repair their carriage door on the Hogwarts Express after Ron slams the door so hard that the window breaks.

REPELLO MUGGLETUM

Latin: repellare - to repel, drive away; repello - I repel, drive away
Muggeltum - all Muggles

This is the Muggle-Repelling Charm. Harry, Ron and Hermione use it in the seventh book, along with other spells, to protect their campsites.

RICTUSEMPRA

Latin: rictus - open mouth; semper - always

This is the Tickling Charm. If a witch or wizard points their wand at another person and says "Rictusempra", the victim starts to laugh uncontrollably.

Harry uses this spell in his second year at Hogwarts when he faces Draco Malfoy at the Duelling Club. Malfoy is hit by a fit of laughter so strong that he falls to his knees.

RIDDIKULUS

from "ridiculous"

This spell is used against Boggarts. Boggarts are magical creatures that take a different form for every person: the form of the thing that each person fears the most. The only way to fight a Boggart is laughter, so the witch or wizard must find a way to make the thing that scares them the most seem ridiculous. If they imagine this ridiculous form and say "Riddikulus", the Boggart is forced to transform into that shape. When it is met by laughter rather than the fear that a Boggart usually causes, the Boggart is stunned. After this has happened multiple times, the Boggart ends up so confused that it disappears.

In the trio's third year at Hogwarts, Defense Against the Dark Arts is taught by Remus Lupin. He teaches Harry and the others this spell. For Harry, the Boggart takes the shape of a Dementor.

Salvio Hexia

Italian: in salvo - safe
Latin: salvus, -a, -um - safe, undamaged
"hex" - a spell

This protective charm protects a place against hexes and minor curses from outside. Hermione, Ron and Harry use it in the seventh book to create a magical shield around their campsite.

Scourgify

"scour" - to scrub clean

"Scourgify" can be used by witches and wizards who don't like cleaning. It makes dirt and dust disappear completely.

The spell is used for the first time by Tonks in the fifth book to clear out Hedwig's cage, although it doesn't work perfectly.

It is also shown in the fifth book what the spell is really capable of. Neville's new plant, *Mimbulus mimbletonia*, sprays Stinksap all over a carriage of the Hogwarts Express, and Ginny uses this spell to clean it up.

SECTUMSEMPRA

Latin: sectum - cut; semper - always

Harry finds this spell with the note "For enemies" in his copy of "Advanced Potion-Making", which belonged to the Half-Blood Prince, but there are no more details about its exact effect. It later turns out that the curse causes deep gashes.

In their sixth year at Hogwarts Harry and Draco Malfoy end up duelling in the boys' toilet. Without knowing its effect, Harry uses this curse against Malfoy. Deep gashes appear on Malfoy's face and chest. Luckily, Professor Snape appears on the scene in time and manages to reduce Malfoy's injuries and take him to the Hospital Wing.

Serpensortia

Latin: serpens - snake; ortus - creation, origin
French: sortir - to come out

The spell "Serpensortia" causes a live snake to shoot out of the tip of a wand.

In their second year Harry faces Draco Malfoy at the Duelling Club and Malfoy uses this spell against Harry. Harry then speaks Parseltongue to the snake that appears, without even realizing it.

SILENCIO

from "silence"

Witches and wizards use this spell to silence other people or creatures. They point their wand at the being and say "Silencio". The victim is then unable to make a noise.

This spell is taught in the fifth year at Hogwarts, and the students practice it on ravens and bullfrogs.

In the same year, Hermione uses it on a Death Eater in the Department of Mysteries to stop him from revealing where they are.

Sonorus

Latin: sonorus - loud, resounding; sonor - sound

If a witch or wizard holds the tip of their wand to their throat and says "Sonorus", their voice is immediately magically amplified as if they are using a megaphone.

At the Quidditch World Cup in the fourth book, Ludo Bagman uses this spell so that all the spectators can hear him – unlike Lee Jordan, he doesn't have a megaphone. To speak at a normal volume again, the counter-charm is "Quietus".

Specialis Revelio

Latin: specialis - particular; specialitas - characteristic, peculiarity; revelare - to reveal
Latin: specialitatem revelo - roughly: I reveal the particular thing / the secret

The spell "Specialis Revelio" is used to reveal the magical properties of an enchanted object. For example, it can be used to reveal hidden text in a book or on parchment.

Professor Snape probably uses a modified version of the spell in the trio's third year at Hogwarts when he says "Reveal your secret" to try and force the Marauder's Map to show its contents. (This doesn't work.)

Hermione also uses it in their sixth year on the copy of "Advanced Potion-Making" that belonged to the Half-Blood Prince. She is trying to find out if there is anything suspicious about it, but like Snape she doesn't succeed.

Stupefy

"stupor" - a daze, numbness
"stupefy" - to numb

The Stunning Spell "Stupefy" makes the person or creature it is used on fall to the floor unconscious.

After the Quidditch World Cup in the fourth book, the house elf Winky is hit by a Stunning Spell. Ministry of Magic employees mistakenly thought she was responsible for the Dark Mark and used the spell to put her out of action.

In the subsequent books, the Stunning Spell is one of the most frequently used spells in the fight against Voldemort's Death Eaters.

To revive a person or creature who has been Stunned using this spell, the counter-charm "Enervate" must be used.

Tarantallegra

Italian: allegro - happy, lively
Tarantella - a folk dance from southern Italy
whose origins are linked to being bitten by a
tarantula

The effect of this curse is similar to the effect of
a tarantula bite. A bite victim begins to shake and
twitch uncontrollably. This curse causes similar
symptoms. The victim loses control of the body
part affected.

At the Duelling Club in their second year Draco
Malfoy uses the Tarantallegra curse on Harry,
whose legs start to dance uncontrollably until he
is freed with the counter-spell "Finite
Incantatem".

Neville is also hit by this curse, in the
Department of Mysteries in the fifth book. A
Death Eater hits him with the spell and Neville
then accidentally destroys the prophecy about
Harry and Voldemort.

TERGEO

Latin: tergere - to clean; tergeo - I clean

This is another cleaning spell. To remove dirt, the witch or wizard points their wand at the spot they want to clean and says "Tergeo" and all of the dirt disappears.

At the beginning of the sixth book Hermione uses this spell to clean the blood off Harry's face after Draco Malfoy breaks his nose.

WADDIWASI

from "wad"

Professor Lupin uses this spell to put a spectacular end to one of Peeves' pranks. The chewing gum that Peeves had stuck in a keyhole shoots out into the poltergeist's nostril.

WINGARDIUM LEVIOSA

Latin: arduum - rising up, high up; levis - light, weightless

One of the first spells taught at Hogwarts is "Wingardium Leviosa", which is used to make objects levitate. But it isn't nearly as easy as it sounds. It is important not only to pronounce the spell correctly while focusing on the object, but also to "swish and flick" the wand. When it is done correctly, the object will start to hover in the air.

In their first year at Hogwarts Hermione is the only one who manages it on her first try in class. But Ron also manages to cast the spell on the same day when Hermione is attacked by a troll. Ron uses the spell to make the troll's club fly up into the air. As the effect wears off, it falls onto the troll's head and knocks it out.

References

The spells as such come from the Harry Potter books 1-7 of author JK Rowling.

Volume 1, Harry Potter and the Sorcerer's Stone, 1997
Volume 2, Harry Potter and the Chamber of Secrets, 1998
Volume 3, Harry Potter and the Prisoner of Azkaban, 1999
Volume 4, Harry Potter and the Goblet of Fire, 2000
Volume 5, Harry Potter and the Order of the Phoenix, 2003
Volume 6, Harry Potter and the Half-Blood Prince, 2005
Volume 7, Harry Potter and the Deathly Hallows 2007

The elaborations of spells declarations by means of different dictionaries for English, Latin and other languages.

The book cover was created by Daniel Boger and includes graphical image elements of freepik.com

Magic hat: www.freepik.com/free-vector/magic-hat_793796.htm

Lightning Source UK Ltd.
Milton Keynes UK
UKOW06f1934011117
312033UK00015B/866/P